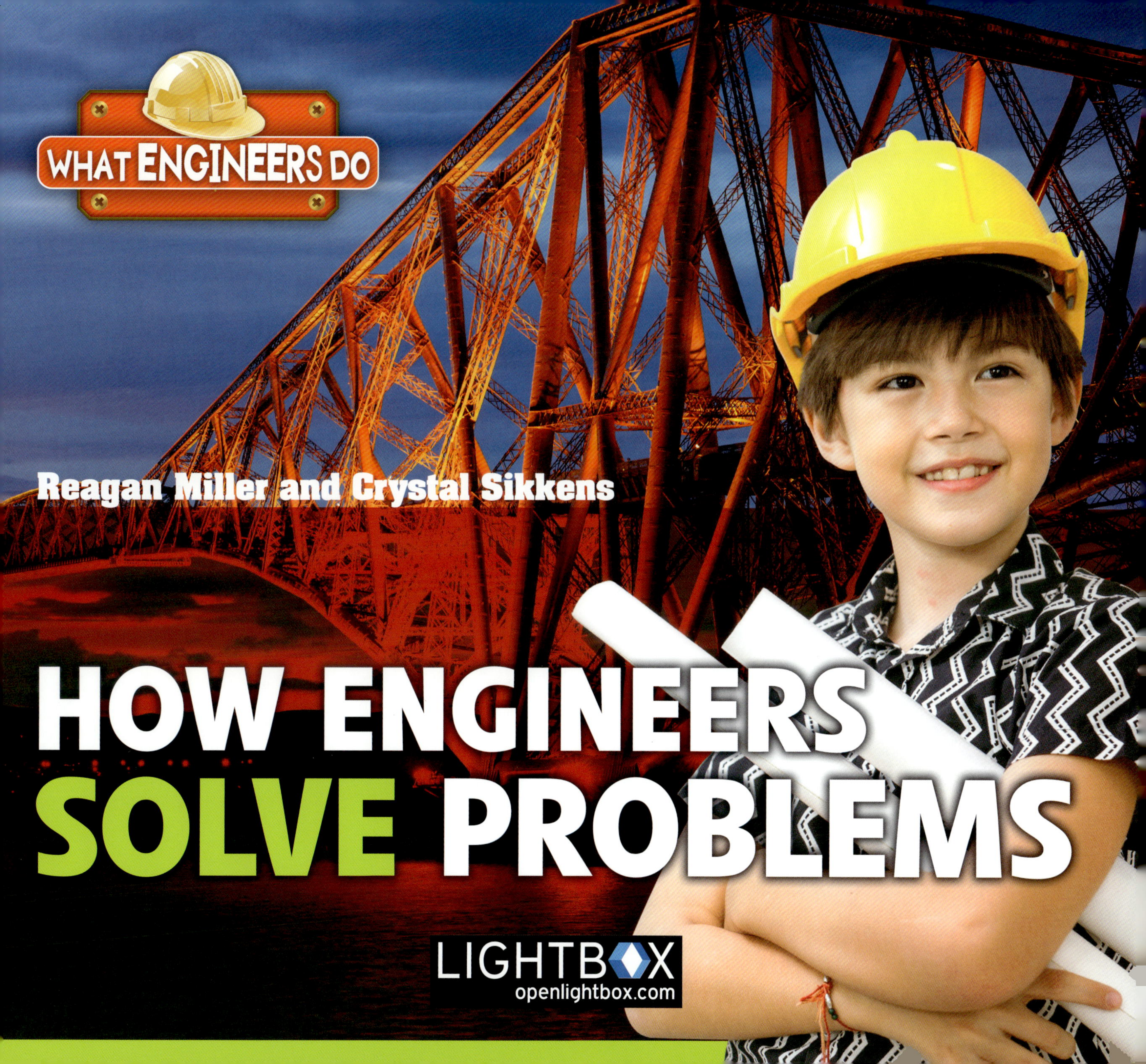
WHAT ENGINEERS DO
Reagan Miller and Crystal Sikkens
HOW ENGINEERS
SOLVE PROBLEMS
LIGHTBOX
openlightbox.com

LIGHTBOX

Go to **www.openlightbox.com** and enter this book's unique code.

ACCESS CODE

LBXH5773

Lightbox is an all-inclusive digital solution for the teaching and learning of curriculum topics in an original, groundbreaking way. Lightbox is based on National Curriculum Standards.

OPTIMIZED FOR

- ✓ TABLETS
- ✓ WHITEBOARDS
- ✓ COMPUTERS
- ✓ AND MUCH MORE!

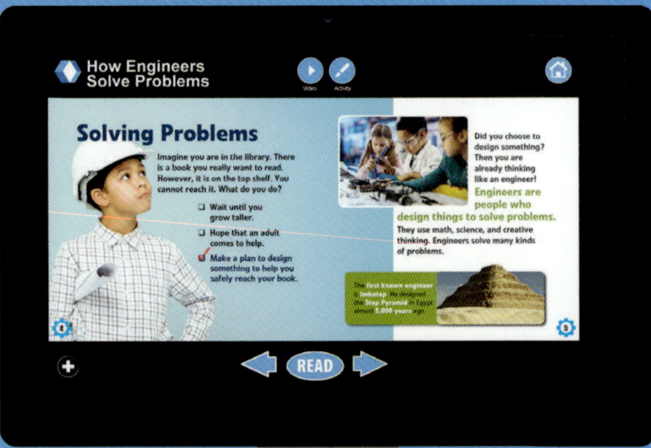

STANDARD FEATURES OF LIGHTBOX

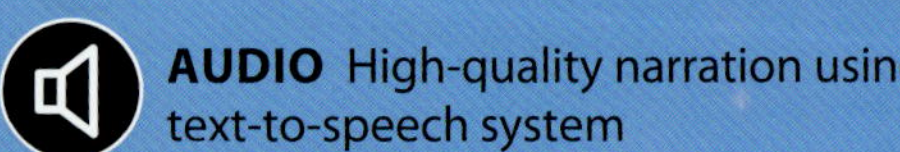

AUDIO High-quality narration using text-to-speech system

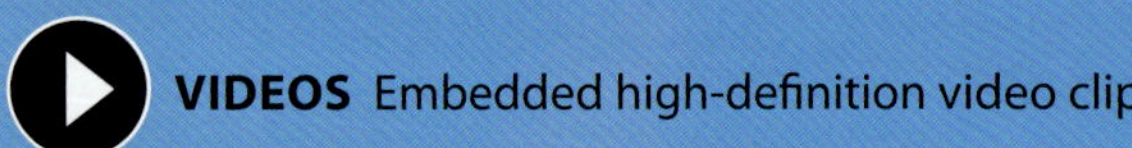

VIDEOS Embedded high-definition video clips

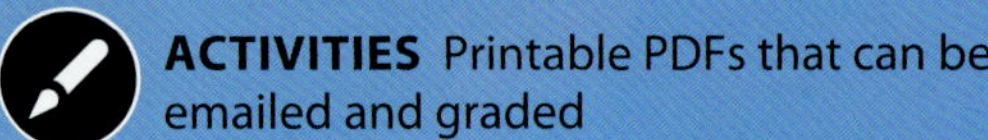

ACTIVITIES Printable PDFs that can be emailed and graded

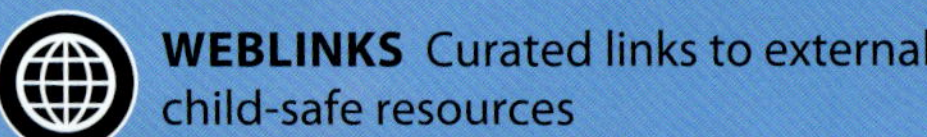

WEBLINKS Curated links to external, child-safe resources

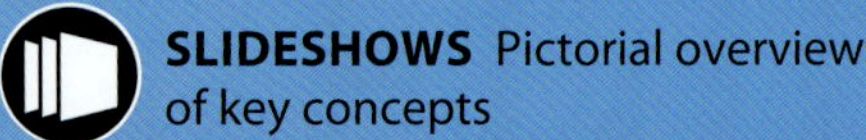

SLIDESHOWS Pictorial overviews of key concepts

INTERACTIVE MAPS Interactive maps and aerial satellite imagery

QUIZZES Ten multiple choice questions that are automatically graded and emailed for teacher assessment

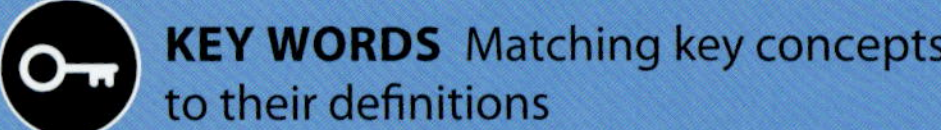

KEY WORDS Matching key concepts to their definitions

VIDEOS

WEBLINKS

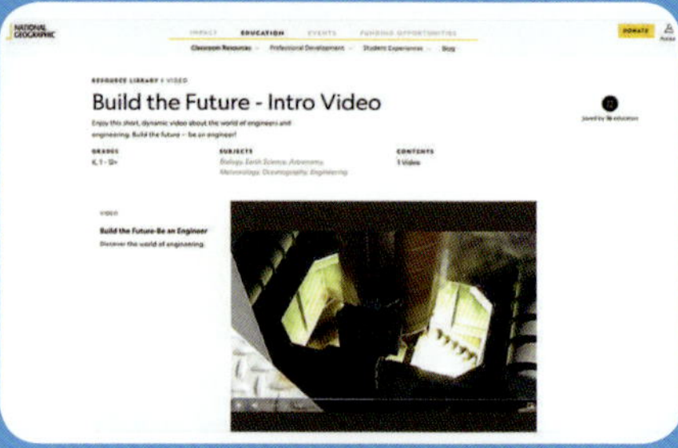

SLIDESHOWS

QUIZZES

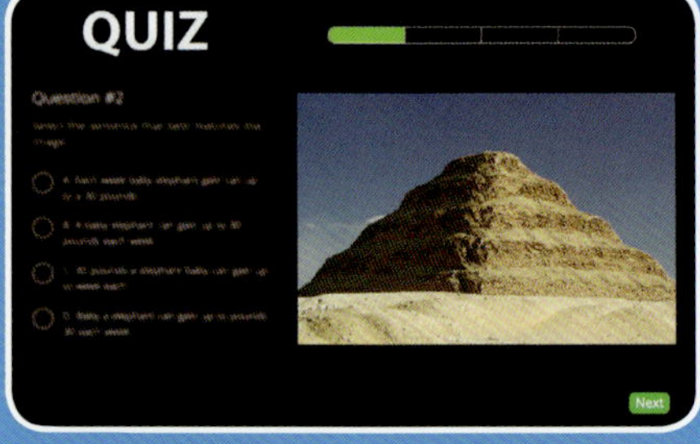

HOW ENGINEERS SOLVE PROBLEMS

Contents

Solving Problems

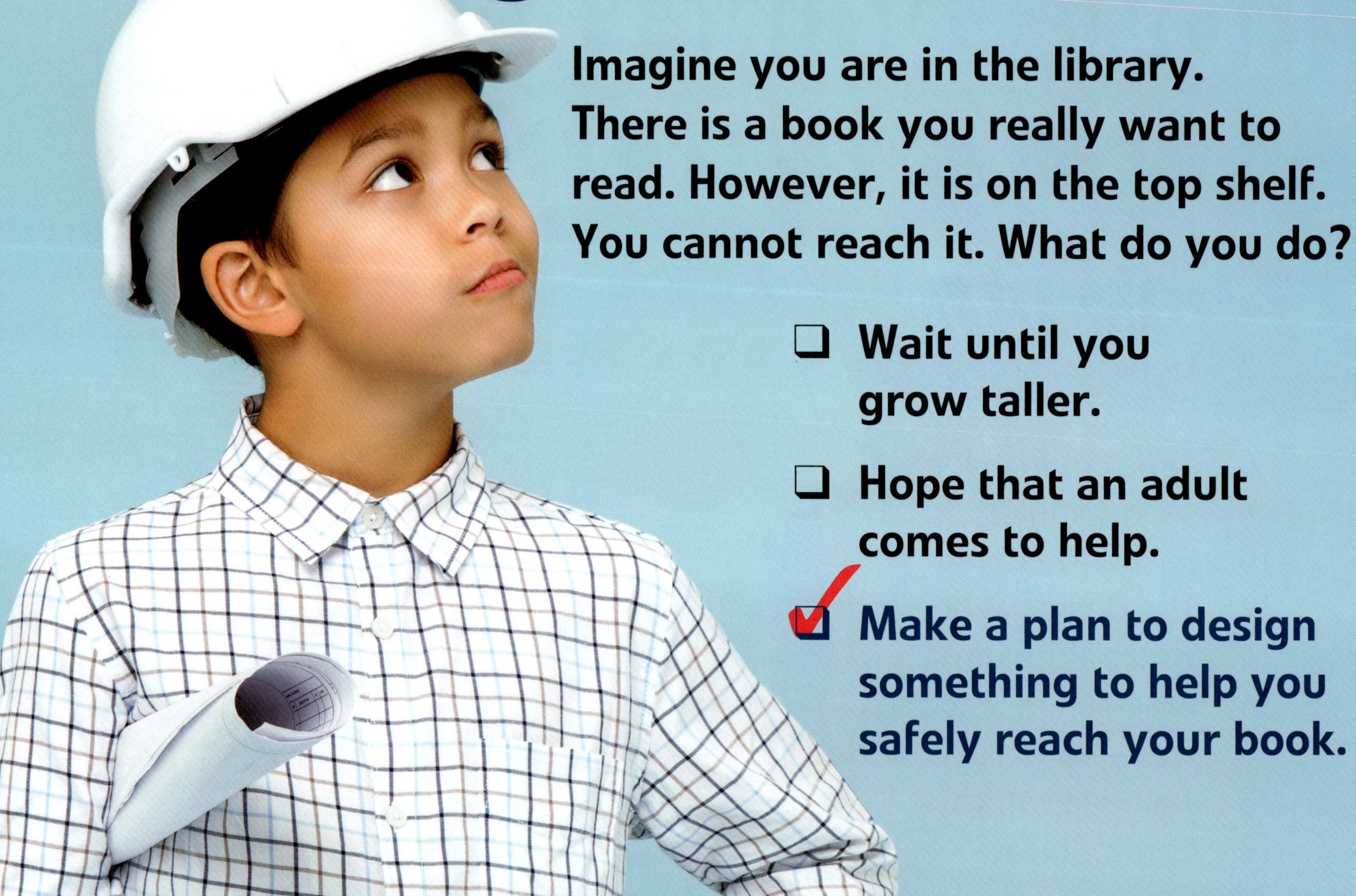

Imagine you are in the library. There is a book you really want to read. However, it is on the top shelf. You cannot reach it. What do you do?

- ❑ Wait until you grow taller.
- ❑ Hope that an adult comes to help.
- ☑ Make a plan to design something to help you safely reach your book.

Did you choose to design something? Then you are already thinking like an engineer!

Engineers are people who design things to solve problems.

They use math, science, and creative thinking. Engineers solve many kinds of problems.

The **first known engineer** was **Imhotep**. He designed the **Step Pyramid of Djoser** in Egypt almost **5,000 years** ago.

Types of Problems

What do you think when you hear the word "problem"? Many people think a problem is something bad. **Engineers are different. They enjoy solving problems.**

There are many types of problems. Different kinds of engineers are needed to solve them. Engineers are professional problem solvers.

Think like an engineer

Think of some problems. Can engineering solve them? What are some things engineers might design?

Technologies

Engineers design many things. The things they design are called technologies. **A technology is anything made by a person to solve a problem or meet a need.**

For example, your pencil might break while you are writing. What do you do now? You use a pencil sharpener. A pencil sharpener is a technology. It solves the problem of your broken pencil.

Think like an engineer

Look at the pictures. Each photograph shows a technology. What problem does each technology solve?

Past and Present

Long ago, people solved problems using simple technologies such as tools. **Tools are objects that people use to make work easier and faster.** There are many different tools. They are made for different kinds of work. Tools help people meet their needs.

Many of our needs today are the same as they were long ago. **Some of the same tools designed long ago are still used today.** However, many work better now. This is because engineers do not just create new technologies. They also improve them.

Think like an engineer

Compare the tools from long ago and today. Can you tell how the tools have improved?

The Design Process

The engineering design process is a set of steps that engineers use as a guide. It helps them find the best solution to a problem.

1 FIND A PROBLEM

Ask questions about the problem to learn about it.

2 BRAINSTORM SOLUTIONS

Work with a group to come up with different ways to solve the problem.

3 PLAN AND MAKE A MODEL

As a group, choose the best solution. Create a plan to make a model of the solution. Gather materials and make your model.

4 TEST AND IMPROVE

Test your model. Record the results. Use the test results to help make your design better. Retest your improved design.

5 COMMUNICATE

Share your design with others.

Find a Problem

Anyone can use the engineering design process. The first step is finding a problem. What are some problems that need to be solved? **Engineers solve problems to help people or the environment.** They may also improve something that is not working.

After engineers have found a problem, they learn about it. They make sure the problem has not already been solved. Then, they gather information. **They may talk to others, ask questions, or do research.** These are all helpful ways to gather information.

Think like an engineer

Can you think of a problem to solve that would help others? Talk to your friends and family. Ask them what problems they would like solved.

Brainstorm Solutions

Once engineers understand the problem, they think about possible solutions. There may be many different solutions to a problem. **Engineers often work as a team.** They work together to find the best solution.

Brainstorming is a group activity used to share ideas. **Engineers use brainstorming to create a list of possible solutions.** When brainstorming, only one person speaks at a time, and everyone else listens. Everyone has a chance to speak. No one judges another person's ideas. All ideas are written down.

Plan and Make a Model

As a group, engineers decide on the best solution to a problem. They must then test the solution. To do this, engineers often build models. **A model is a representation of a real object. Models show how something will look.** They can also show how different parts of an object work together. A model can be solid and three-dimensional, or it may be a drawing or diagram instead.

Test and Improve

A model is not the real object. It may not have all the same parts or details. However, it can help people understand the engineer's idea. **Testing a model is a good way to see whether an idea will work.** It can also tell an engineer what needs to be fixed or changed.

Communicate

What happens once a problem is solved? Engineers communicate their design. **They share their solution with the world.** Models help them explain their solution. The problem is then solved for other people, too.

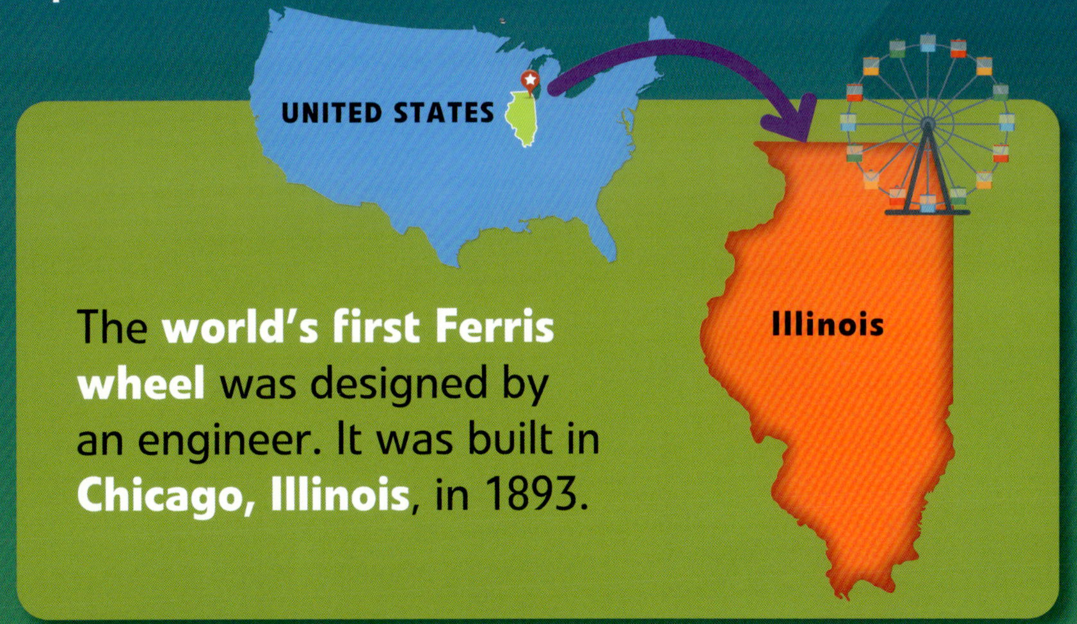

The **world's first Ferris wheel** was designed by an engineer. It was built in **Chicago, Illinois**, in 1893.

Problem-Solving Kids

Anyone can become an engineer! **Kids just like you have designed technologies to solve problems.** Cassidy Goldstein designed a holder for broken crayons. She was 11 years old.

In 1873, Chester Greenwood invented earmuffs. He was 15 years old. Chester wanted to keep his ears warm while ice skating. He designed earmuffs to solve his problem. His solution helped others, too.

An **11-year-old** boy invented the **Popsicle** in **1905**.

ACTIVITY

Solve a Problem

The world is full of problems waiting to be solved. You can solve problems, too! Just follow the steps of the engineering design process.

There is always more than one solution to a problem. **Different objects can be designed to solve the same problem.** Testing models helps you see which object works best.

1 Think of a problem to solve. It could help people, animals, or the environment. Here are some ideas to get you started.

- Design a tool to peel an orange without getting sticky hands.
- Find a safe way to pick up garbage. This will help keep the environment clean.

2 Brainstorm solutions with a group. Choose the two best solutions together.

3 Create a plan to make a model for each solution. Collect the materials you need. Build the two models.

4 Test both models. Record the results. Compare their strengths and weaknesses. Which model worked better?

5 Share your design with your friends and classmates.

KEY WORDS

Research has shown that as much as 65 percent of all written material published in English is made up of 300 words. These 300 words cannot be taught using pictures or learned by sounding them out. They must be recognized by sight. This book contains 130 common sight words to help young readers improve their reading fluency and comprehension. This book also teaches young readers several important content words, such as proper nouns. These words are paired with pictures to aid in learning and improve understanding.

Page	Sight Words First Appearance
4	a, an, are, book, comes, do, grow, help, in, is, it, make, on, read, really, something, that, the, there, to, until, want, what, you, your
5	almost, and, did, first, he, kinds, like, many, of, people, then, they, things, use, was, who, years
6	different, hear, them, think, when, word
7	can, might, some
8	by, example, for, made, need, now, or, while
9	at, does, each, look, pictures, shows
10	also, as, because, just, long, new, not, our, same, still, such, their, this, were, work
11	from, have, how, tell
12	about, ask, find, group, learn, set, up, ways, with
13	others
14	after, all, be, been, found, has, may, talk, these
15	family, would
16	another, down, ideas, list, no, often, once, one, only, time, together
17	must, parts, three, too, will
18	good, see, states
19	world
20	old, she
21	boy, his, keep

Page	Content Words First Appearance
4	adult, library, plan, problems, shelf
5	Egypt, engineer, Imhotep, math, science, Step Pyramid of Djoser
7	engineering
8	pencil, pencil sharpener, person, technologies
9	photograph
10	objects, past, present, tools
12	engineering design process, questions, solution, steps
13	materials, model, results
14	environment, information, research
15	friends
16	activity, brainstorming, chance, team
17	diagram, drawing, representation
18	details
19	Chicago, Ferris Wheel, Illinois
20	Cassidy Goldstein, crayons, holder, kids, United States
21	Chester Greenwood, earmuffs, ears, ice skating, Popsicle

Published by Smartbook Media Inc.
14 Penn Plaza, 9th Floor New York, NY 10122
Website: www.openlightbox.com

Library of Congress Control Number: 2020936987

ISBN 978-1-5105-5414-6 (hardcover)
ISBN 978-1-5105-5415-3 (multi-user eBook)

Printed in Guangzhou, China
1 2 3 4 5 6 7 8 9 0 24 23 22 21 20

052020
110819

Project Coordinator: Priyanka Das
Designer: Jean Faye Marie Rodriguez

Every reasonable effort has been made to trace ownership and to obtain permission to reprint copyright material. The publisher would be pleased to have any errors or omissions brought to its attention so that they may be corrected in subsequent printings.

The publisher acknowledges Getty Images, iStock, and Shutterstock as the primary image suppliers for this title.

First published by Crabtree Publishing Company in 2014.